THE A TO Z BOOK OF TEXAS WILDFLOWERS

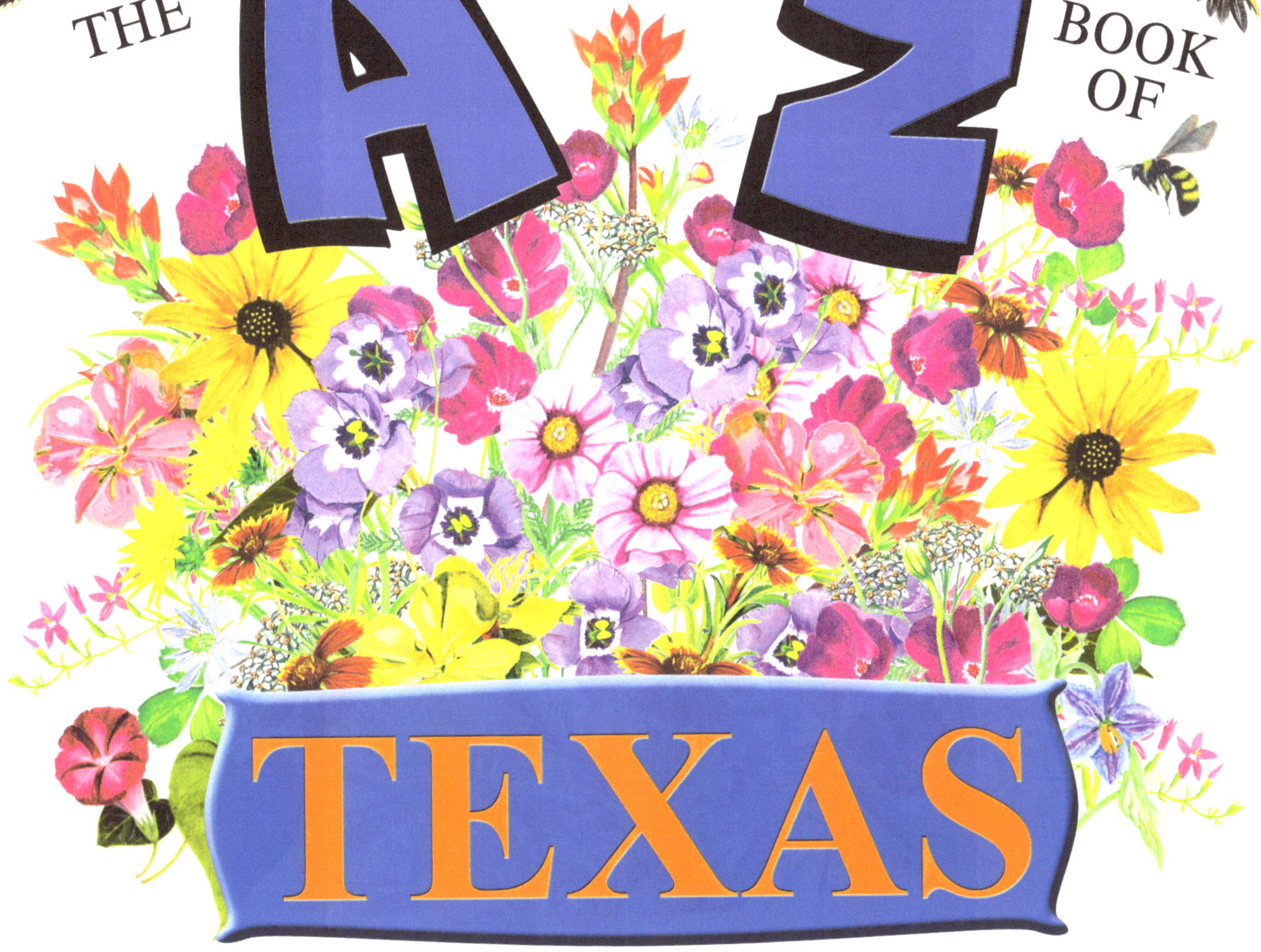

To Arthur, Enjoy the Hunt! Kathy J Shields 2025

Kathleen J. Shields   Michael P. Earney

Special thanks to
Susan Sander with the
Riverside Nature Center in Kerrville, Texas,

Joe Marcus at the Ladybird Johnson
Flower Center in Austin, Texas, and

Kathleen's Graphics for her tireless dedication
in making this book and book cover look so good.

No part of this publication may be reproduced, stored in a retrieval system or transmitted in any way by any means, electronic, mechanical, photocopy, recording or otherwise without the prior permission of the author except as provided by USA copyright law.

© Copyright 2025 "The A to Z of Texas Wildflowers for Kids"
by Kathleen J. Shields & Michael P. Earney - All rights reserved.

ISBN-13: 978-1-956581-64-5 **Hardback**
ISBN-13: 978-1-956581-65-2 **Paperback**

Acrylic Illustrations by: Michael P. Earney
Cover Graphics by Kathleen's Graphics

Canyon Lake, Texas
www.ErinGoBraghPublishing.com

It's springtime here in Texas, y'all,
and with a gully washer or two...

Magical colors
will paint the fields,
it's quite a sight to view!

Deep in the Heart of Texas,
just past the concrete road,
You'll see wild blooms a-sproutin'
- *if the grass ain't been mowed.*

The countryside is blooming, while the wind makes colors sway,
Let's hunt for Texas wildflowers,
where the deer and the Antelope *horn* play.

And why are these flowers special, beyond the way they grew?
Well darlin' these are Texan! Come on – I'll show you, too.

If flowers could talk,
they'd never stop,
they have
so much
to share!

So pause a spell and breathe it in
— that sweetness in the air.

There are flowers you can cook with,
and some that help you heal.
Flowers shaped like trumpets,
and some shaped like a wheel.

They feed the birds and butterflies,
the bees need them to thrive.
The hummingbirds drink nectar,
keepin' the hills alive!

So grab yer boots and cowboy hat,
a camera and this book…
Let's head out to the countryside,
and take a closer look!

With bluebonnets and paintbrushes,
and sunflowers tall and wide,
You'll learn the names, the stories too —
a Texas bouquet with pride!

Kathleen J. Shields & Michael P. Earney - 2025

A is for ANTELOPE HORN

*VIP: Very Important Plant!

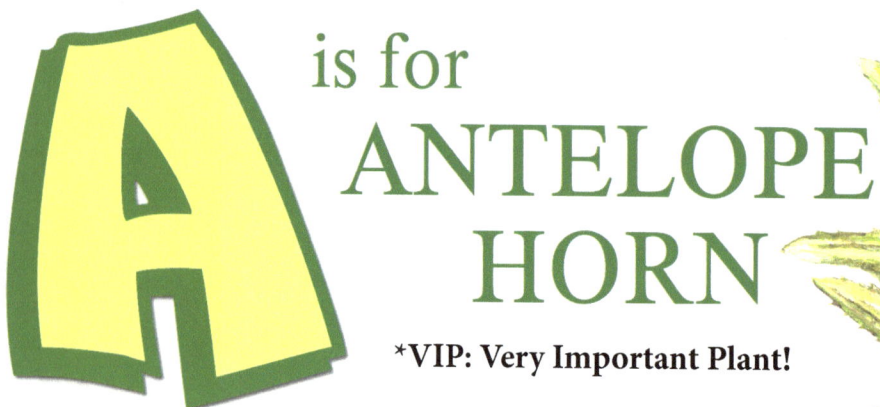

A Very Important Plant is the Antelope Horn. It's the only place Monarch Butterfly are ever born!

With twisting stems and blooms so neat, This Texas flower is hard to beat!

Antelope Horn is a type of milkweed where monarch butterflies lay their eggs. Its sticky, poisonous sap is one of the only things monarch caterpillars can eat. The poison doesn't hurt them, but it makes them taste bad, so predators stay away. If there's no milkweed, monarchs can't lay eggs, caterpillars can't grow, and the butterflies lose their protection. Without Antelope Horn, monarchs could go extinct! Let them grow—don't mow.

B is for BLUEBONNET

**With petals blue and tops of white,
Their blooms in fields are quite a sight.
They're picture perfect, will make you glow.
* But don't you pick them, let them grow!**

* Bluebonnets are the State Flower of Texas and are illegal to pick.

C is for CHOLLA

**A blooming cactus that likes it hot
found in deserts, in a sunny spot.**

**Some birds like Wren make it a home.
Safe in there, while predator's roam.**

D is for DANDELION

A sleepy flower, at night will yawn,
and close up tight until the dawn.

From yellow blooms
to fluffs of white,
they catch a breeze
and then take flight.

F is for Firewheel
aka Indian Blanket

A painted flower
of yellows and reds,
This Indian Blanket
has 'petal' threads.

Blooms through summer
as it loves the sun.

This native flower
is really fun.

H is for HONEYSUCKLE

Fragrant scent
with drops of nectar.
Twisting vines,
make it look better.

Colorful blooms
that boldly say;
Bees and butterflies,
come and play.

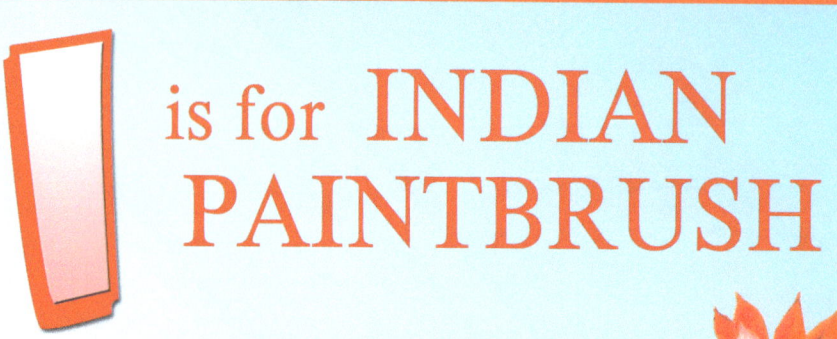

I is for INDIAN PAINTBRUSH

A flower with no petals, just bracts that look like fall.

Red and orange colors, these flowers can grow tall.

In Native American culture, they represent the West.

Symbols of strength and beauty, these flowers are the best.

*Bracts are special leaves that grow near flowers. They are often colorful and can look like petals, but they're not the real flowers. Bracts help attract pollinators like bees and butterflies.

J is for JOHNNY JUMP-UP

Johnny Jump-ups, are quick to grow.
Their colorful petals steal the show.
Purple, yellow and white, with cheer,
It jumps up fast when spring is near.

K is for
KNIGHT's MILFOIL
aka yarrow

This yarrow plant has many names, and its uses have medicinal claims.

A curing plant, a historical fave. Once used for wounds by knights so brave.

L is for LANTANA

This bush can bloom
in all four seasons.
Don't eat the berries,
for toxic reasons.

Colored flowers
change as they age,
Yellow, pink, orange –
they're all the rage.

M is for MORNING GLORY

Funnel shaped flowers on vines that climb.

They'll cover a fence in record time.

Bright colors like blue, purple, pink and white,
They even can bloom in colored stripe!

N is for NIGHTSHADE

A mysterious name
with a spooky sound.

With star-shaped flowers
close to the ground.

Grows in gardens, fields,
and wooded cover.

Be warned—it tends to take right over!

 is for

OXEYE DAISY

Why does a flower, small and bright, Take its name from an ox's sight?

A tiny bloom that loves to grow, Maybe we will never know.

P is for PRICKLY PEAR

**Its pads are flat
with spines so sharp,
Its blooms are bright, a work of art.**

**And when they turn to fruit, you'll see:
A feast for wildlife, and for me.**

Q is for QUEEN ANNE'S LACE

**Named for the royal
patterned clothes.**

**Growing wild
along the roads.**

**It may look pretty,
but do not eat,
it could be poison,
it's not a treat.**

R is for REDBUD

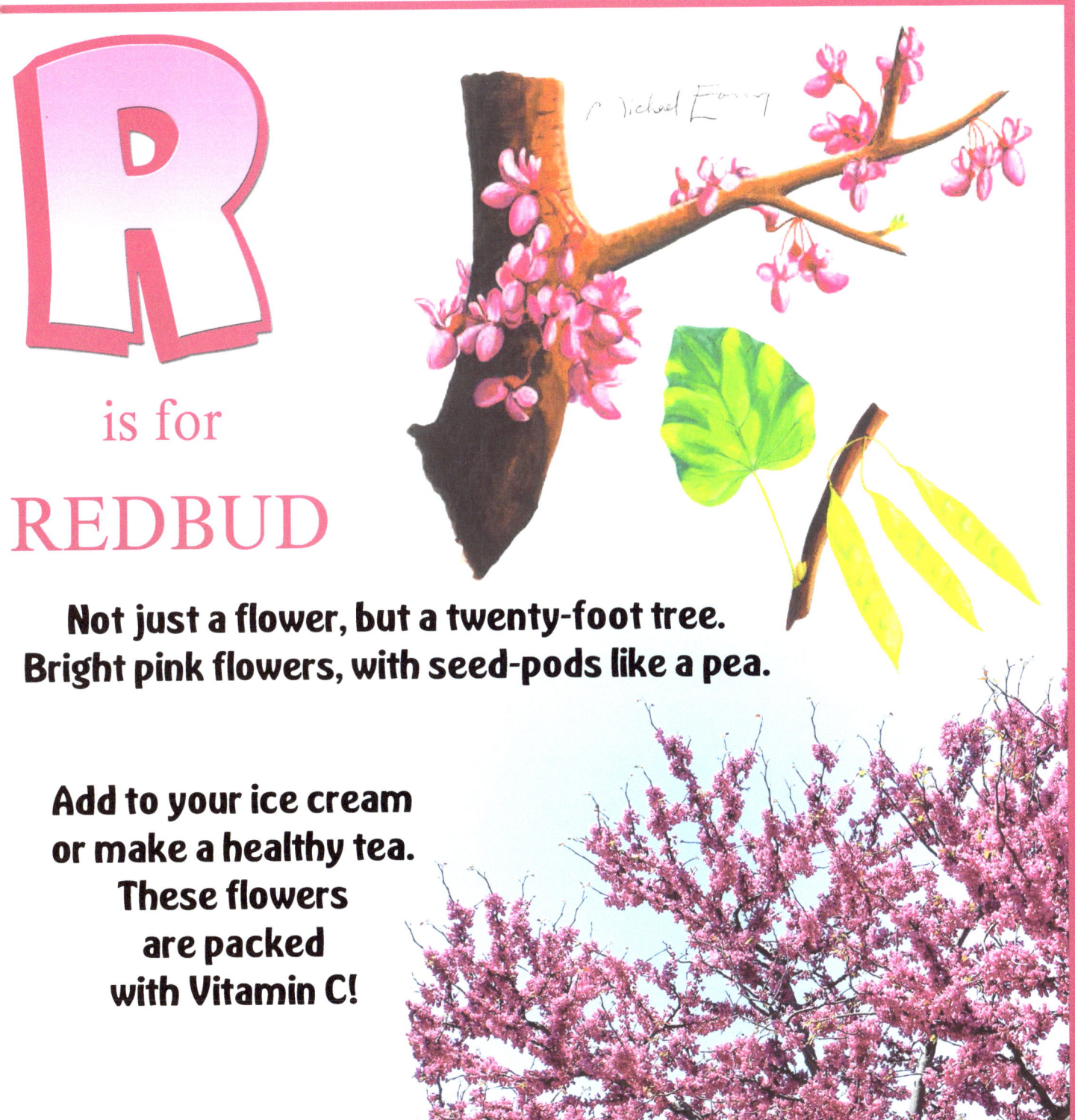

**Not just a flower, but a twenty-foot tree.
Bright pink flowers, with seed-pods like a pea.**

**Add to your ice cream
or make a healthy tea.
These flowers
are packed
with Vitamin C!**

S is for SUNFLOWER

They're super tall,
three times your height!
With seeds that pack
a healthy delight.

Young flower heads turn to face the sun,
Standing proud till the day is done.

T is for TRUMPET VINE

With tubular blooms
 like a trumpet horn,
  This fast-growing vine,
   wakes with the morn.

Climbing high
 where soft breezes swirl.
It draws in hummingbirds,
 their wings all a-twirl.

U is for UNICORN HORN

A unique flower that can't be missed, With hard seed pods, that spiral and twist.

So if you spot one stop and stare! Just don't pick them since they're rare.

V is for VERBENA

**From spring to fall, they bloom so long,
A party for pollinators, with a buzzing song.**

**Cascading blooms,
scent fills the air,
Attracting butterflies
everywhere.**

W is for WINE-CUP

A unique cup shape,
has earned their name.

Returning each year,
always the same.

Self-seeding,
spreading,
they fill the space.

Needing little water,
they find their place.

X is for
Xanthisma texanum
Sleepy Daisy

When the sun goes down
making darkened skies.
They close their blooms
as you close your eyes.

Small bright flowers,
with petals like rays,
Make this a favorite
on hot summer days.

y is for YUCCA

An agave plant with
sword-like leaves,
Storing energy
until it breathes.

But when the stalk
starts to stretch up high,
stand back and watch
as flowers touch
the sky!

Z is for

Zeltnera beyrichii
Mountain Pink

While this flower's name starts with a Z,
It's common name, fits it perfectly.

Growing near mountains and high elevation,
These pink floral blooms, are a sensation.

ANEMONE

BLUEBELL

That was just the start
of the blooms that can be found.
You'll discover many more flowers,
if you look around.

The Anemone, a bonus,
it's blooms stands tall and thin.
Another name for her
is the Daughter of the Wind

The Bluebell's shape is bell-like,
but their petals do not ring.
Yet these pretty little things,
will be dancing in the spring.

The Mexican Hat has a shape
that looks like a sombrero.
A flower fiesta, that says;
¡Hola, soy la flor del campo!

Hola = Hello | Soy la Flor = I am the Flower | Del campo = Of the field

MEXICAN HAT

FOXGLOVE

The Foxglove has a folk-lore
about fairies and a fox,
Sneaking into chicken coops,
to feast on sleeping flocks.

The Jimson Weed
may look quite nice,
but trouble's what it brings.
It fooled the Brits in Jamestown,
and caused some dreadful things!

What other flowers can you spot?
Can you find them all?

Impress your friends and family,
when you name them, y'all!

JIMSON WEED

Kathleen J. Shields

has won multiple book awards for her Inspirational and Educational Children's stories.

"The Hamilton Troll Adventures"

"The First Unicorn" and

"The First UniBear"

Learn more at
www.KathleensBooks.com

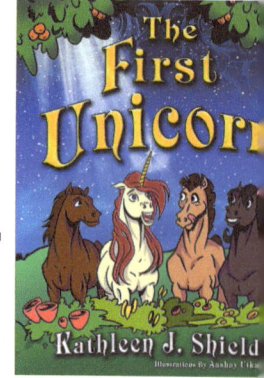

CHRISTIAN STORIES

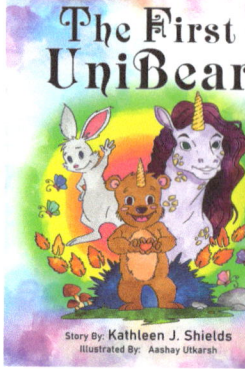

 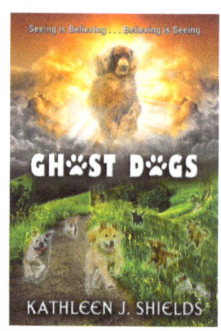 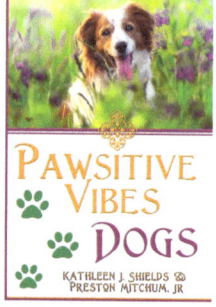  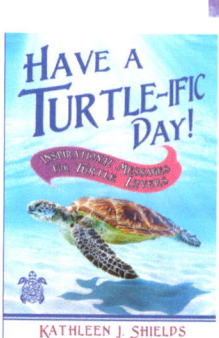 

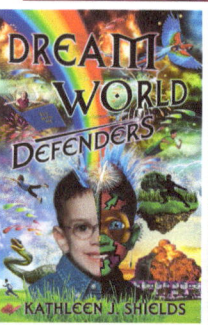 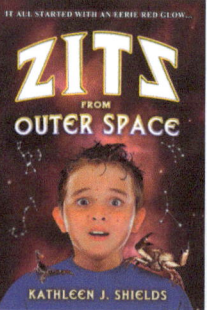 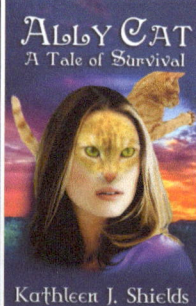  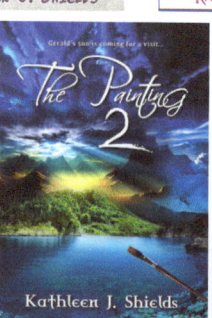  

Michael P. Earney is a renowned fine arts painter and has been a commercial artist, ceramic sculptor, a potter, an award-winning documentary filmmaker and published author of numerous works.

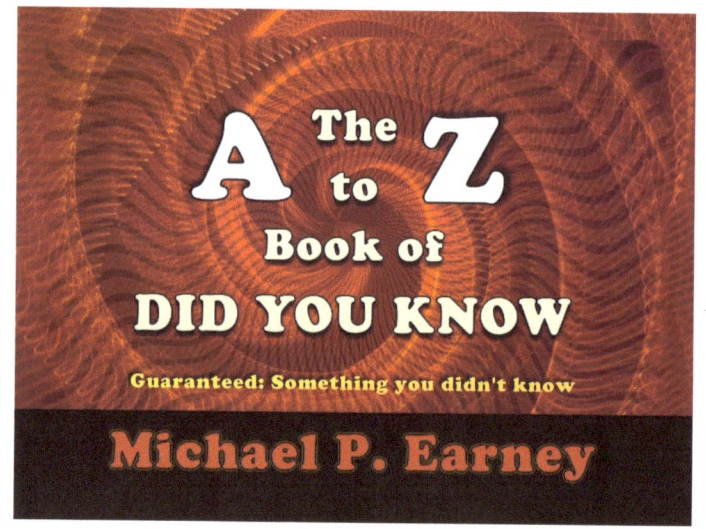

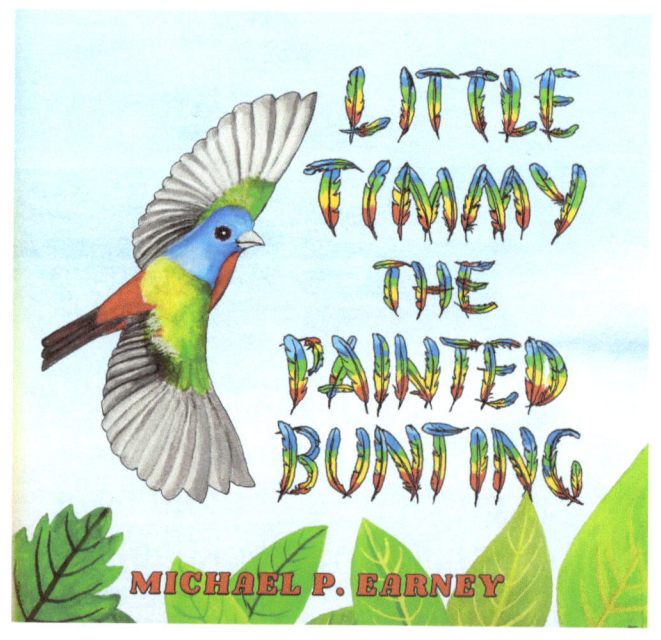

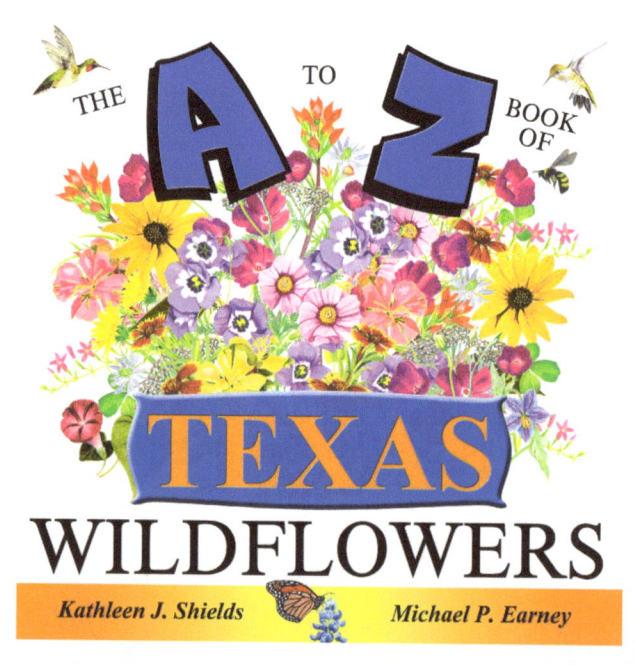

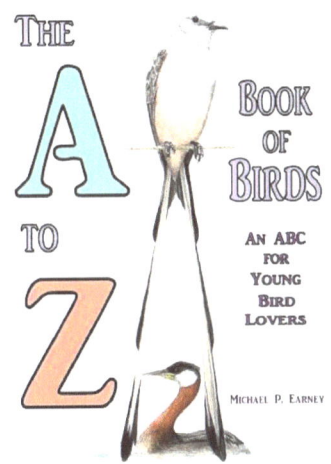
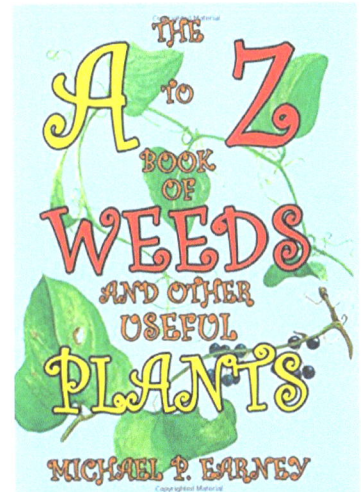
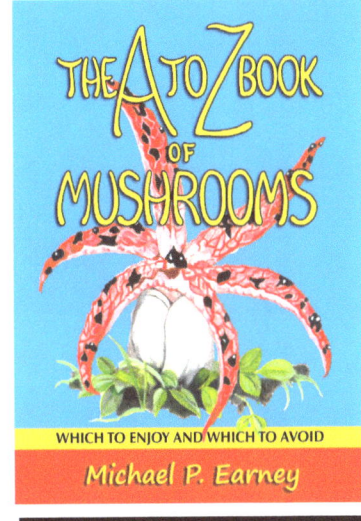

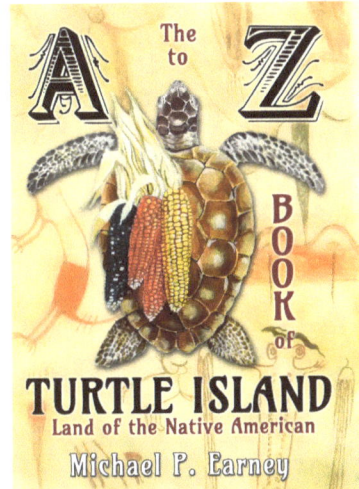
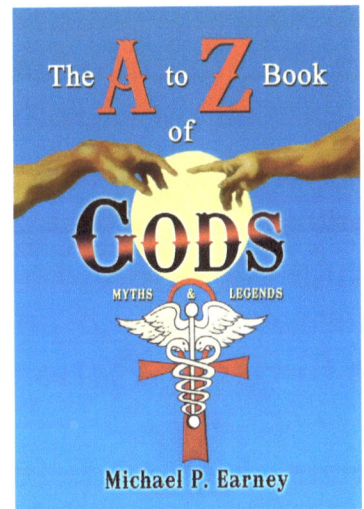
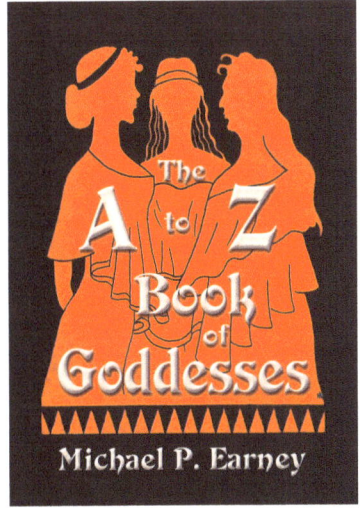

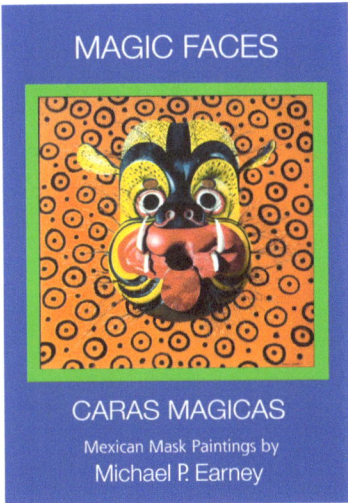

ERIN GO BRAGH
Publishing

Erin Go Bragh Publishing publishes various genres of books for numerous authors. Their portfolio consists of a 1200-page Vietnamese to English Dictionary, Historical fiction, an award-winning children's educational series, multiple adult novels and memoirs, tween adventure stories, poetry as well as Christian Fiction for all ages.

Their objective is to promote literacy and education through reading and writing.

www.ErinGoBraghPublishing.com
Canyon Lake, Texas

www.ingramcontent.com/pod-product-compliance
Lightning Source LLC
LaVergne TN
LVHW071118151025
822843LV00007B/85